MY SOUL IS A WITNESS

Poetry By

YECHEILYAH YSRAYL

Yecheilyah Ysrayl

yecheilyah@yecheilyahysrayl.com

www.yecheilyahysrayl.com

Cover Design by: Prudence Makhura

Edited by: Eva Xan

First Edition 2020

CONTENTS

A POEM IS BORN

Not all poems are conceived in light.

Some of them are buried in darkness,

surrounded by dirt and soil,

gritted teeth

and clenched fists.

Sometimes, the lyric is a resurrection of rage,

a fire that is only quenched through spilled ink

on blank pages.

Sometimes, poems are tears,

because not all compositions

are conceived

in well-lit rooms.

Some poems are seeds that only grow in darkness—

Or did you not know that is how seeds grow?

Hidden, covered, and planted in the dirt,

the sun coming in from someplace outside of itself,

Yecheilyah Ysrayl

water pouring in from someplace outside of itself.

Some sonnets are crushed grapes,

crumpled and left for dead—

Or did you not know that is how wine is made?

Something fermenting,

festering and developing

into something worse.

Some poems are nearly dead

before they reach the light—

Or did you not know that is how the Messiah rose?

From the grave,

from the pit,

from the earth.

When you feel that you cannot write,

that your life is a laughing contradiction

thrown back into your face,

a joke everyone gets but you;

when your hands tremble with uncertainty

too weak to hold the pen

and too fragile to unvirgin the page,

write anyway.

Because not all poems are conceived in light.

Some of them, the *best* of them,

are buried in darkness

and covered in dirt

until suddenly,

like a sprouting seed,

a poem is born.

SHE IS

She is Neo-Soul

and Conscious Rap.

Negro Spirituals

and Motown.

She is a jagged edge

and digital underground.

Stockley Carmichael

and Steve Coakley.

Tupac *and* Biggie.

Kweli *and* Jay-Z.

Martin *and* Malcolm.

Tubman *and* Truth.

She is Luther Vandross *and* Jaheim

Destiny's Child *and* SWV.

She is no newborn

and neither is she ancient.

Her mind is both fresh and seasoned,

experienced and innocent.

She does not fit in, nor does she try.

The world is not big enough

to shelf

her light.

She is MC.

Her taste,

Souls of Mischief.

She is a timeless prayer

and worth far more than rubies.

She Mos Def does not seek to be understood

by people already committed to misunderstanding

her vibes, which

are not up for debate.

She is classic literature

and urban fiction.

She does not waver.

She does not fold.

She is

an old soul.

I WANT MY STUFF

I want my truth before slavery.

I want customs and traditions

without being conditioned.

I want unconditioned hair.

I want my stuff.

I want my Kings and Queens,

my silver and my gold

I want my laws and commandments

and my stories retold.

I want do-overs

for how we have been done over.

I want my children re-educated.

Give me raised fists

and two-parent households.

I want functioning Black family units,

Afros, Black Power, curly hair,

and I want my cocoa butter skin.

I want credit for all my skills.

I want my midwives.

I want my tribes.

I want my inventions before you re-invented them.

I want Lewis Howard Latimer, not Thomas Edison.

I want my covenants renewed.

I want my 40 acres and a mule.

I want my land as fertile as I left it.

I want my spirituality accepted.

I want my names changed back.

I want my Proverbs and freedom songs,

and I want my Moses Black.

I want what you stole from me.

I want King Solomon Black and comely.

I want it all back.

I want my stuff.

COURAGE

How dramatic the transformation is

when you turn into lioness.

How dangerous courage is,

but how beautiful too.

How tingly the feeling is

when you throw caution to the wind.

When an introvert speaks,

you know that little mustard seed's got fire.

How revolutionary it is to be humble in spirit,

but courageous in character.

The weight of this bravery,

both heavy and powerful.

How sensitive and warrior-like

you are at the same time.

How powerful the strength is

when you do not know that it is there.

WE ARE NOT NEGROES

———— ❦ ————

Negroes are born without a name and without a record.

They are boys despite age,

Uncles and Johns.

Your Negroes are sign language,

using symbols to communicate their existence.

They are born without land,

without placement,

without ownership.

What Dr. King referred to as "a degeneration of nobodyness."

They are sojourners wandering from person to person

in search of themselves.

Your Negroes are born without heritage,

without honor,

without pride,

without mothers—

their umbilical cords cut,

their screams muffled with injustice,

their bodies sold, and their bellies stuffed with lies.

Your Negroes bleed death

and cannot recognize their own corpse.

But we are not your Negroes.

We are soil and Earth.

Lips that sing, mouths and song and praise.

We are bodies and flesh,

veins and blood, and saltwater.

We are water, nurturing, and strong.

We are crowns and rubies and pearls,

eyes and nose, vision, and smell.

We are scripture and fire and dripping honey.

We are blood, teeth, and bone.

We are a people brave.

Proud.

Strong.

But we are not your Negroes.

ADDICT

Your scent lingers long after you have gone.

I breathe you in,

intoxicated by the integrity

of your soul.

You leave, and I lay in bed,

inhaling your spirit.

Anxious for a whiff of your mind,

hungry for a sip of your wisdom,

dazed by the intellect of the lyrics

you spew so effortlessly.

I'm an addict for your words.

The conversation is an intimacy

deeper than penetration.

All these years,

and we are closer

than when we first met.

THE YEAR OF "THE LAUNCH"

Creating, launching, publishing.

It was the year of "The Launch."

In 2020, the world ended.

Our comforts, our safety-nets, our guarantees.

We needed to start something to preserve our sanity.

The big IT, whatever IT was…

The word we chose was PRODUCTIVE.

Everyone needed to produce. Manufacture. Construct.

"Start a business," we said.

"Launch a podcast," we said

"Write a book," we said.

"If you come out of this with nothing new,

shame on you," we said.

We shamed those who sat on their hands.

"Produce, produce, produce!"

"Do more."

It was 2020, but it felt like *1984*.

We needed new beginnings.

The only problem was no one considered endings:

Ending hatred.

Ending homelessness.

Ending strife.

Ending sorrow.

Ending bigotry.

Ending war.

In 2020, our world ended,

and the words we chose to cope with

were "being productive."

Except, we forgot to produce

better versions of ourselves.

THE BLACK PLAGUE

They treated them like The Black Plague,

this walking pestilence ravaging the Earth.

Walking all proud and powerful,

all royalty-like and purposeful,

infecting generations of people with its culture,

music, dance, and cornrolls.

This was a virus that needed to be controlled.

They could not have this thing infecting people with all this hope.

COVID-19 is terrifying, but empowering the people was worse

so, the powers that be raised their glasses smiled

and solidified the oath.

The first phase was overt.

Strip them of their names, rape their wives,

and remove their clothes.

Next, shackle them together and dismantle their dignity.

The vaccination was so far working.

They became Mammies instead of Mothers

and Negroes instead of Kings.

But the Black Plague continued to spread.

It continued to influence

and shift the direction of the Earth.

There was no restraining the wind,

and out of its affliction, grew the epidemic

of black excellence.

Building communities, gaining wealth, and reestablishing identity.

The so-called powers had to take their power back

and so, they infected their neighborhoods with crack.

Mass incarcerate them,

"Jump Jim Crow" them,

redline them,

school-to-prison pipeline them,

hide their history,

hide their truth,

miseducate them and kill the youth.

Put your knees on their necks

and stick your knives in their backs—

But none of it worked.

It was a secret deeper than White Supremacy,

more in-depth than the witchcraft of stolen identity,

deeper than unarmed black men bleeding on the streets,

more frightening than charred bodies hanging from trees.

More detailed than this apparent sickness was the truth:

These people they called plagues were not plagues at all,

they were Prophets

and healers of the Earth.

It was no wonder that,

the more they were afflicted,

the more they grew.

TO BE LOVED

Every living thing wants to be loved.

We need it like the lyrics in our throats

when the beat drops

on our favorite song,

like the natural way our bones jump

and our legs twitch

and our hands move about

as we dance.

Every living thing needs to be loved,

like dandelions in a field trying to convince the world

that they are not just weeds.

We hope someone will care enough to watch over us

and not transgress our boundaries,

will not severe our flowers from their roots,

will not pluck our souls

from their skin.

Yecheilyah Ysrayl

We do not need to be picked and fussed over.

We hope only to be loved,

to be cared about while breath

still feeds our lungs.

Hoping someone will love us intentionally,

like the giggles of a child—

free, raw, and innocent.

We hope to be as valuable as the swell

of a woman's womb,

the protruding belly that everyone wants to touch,

but no one does without permission.

The delicate miracle we all want to protect,

and we hope to be miracles too,

a surprising welcome worthy of protection

because every living thing

wants to be loved.

THE WEIGHT OF WRITING

The weight of what we write.

The ability to influence the direction of a decision,

to direct the path of someone's life for better or for worse.

The responsibility of altering a person's state of mind.

Isn't it blood on our hands if we do it wrong?

People watch and people mimic.

Can we be counted on to be saviors and not devils?

Heavy is the pen.

This is the weight of writing.

REMIND YOURSELF THAT YOU EXIST

When your hands are shaking so badly

and your body is an earthquake;

When your mind is a warzone of worry;

When uncertainty is an uninvited guest,

snaking its way inside your mind

and poisoning it with doubt;

When you are weighed down by

what is not yours to carry;

When depression feels like a friend

and sadness a sister,

remind yourself that you exist.

Don't you know purpose entered your lungs,

armed and ready for battle?

The universe waits for you with unparalleled patience,

accepting delay and

tolerating suffering.

It waits for you with a vase for your tears

and an embrace for your misunderstanding.

Remember how your bones were formed

and stitched together inside someone else's body.

Remember that you are a miracle,

a divine welcome.

Your mother and father's prophecy,

a spiritual alliance of their passion,

their history in one body.

You are history—

soil and earth,

a timeless treasure.

Purpose waits for you

to find the courage to see yourself

because you exist.

You take up space,

you send energy out into the world,

you vibrate at a frequency that someone else feels,

you speak a language that someone else understands.

Yecheilyah Ysrayl

You are the manifestation of love,

and the universe commands that you jump,

even when your heart is in your throat,

because you are here.

Remind yourself that you

exist.

GRIEF

It came in waves today.

Grief did.

The sound of Yolanda Adams

opening her heart

did it.

I was wrong to listen.

Her voice was a gun,

her lyrics a trigger,

and me, the victim.

She was thunder

and my tears, rain.

Yolanda knows I can't listen to that song.

It hoola hooped on the radio in'99,

the year we lived with him

and I combed my Barbie's hair to her voice

as my Dad's memory rode on the backs of those lyrics.

A warrior,

Yecheilyah Ysrayl

the knight in shining armor

of my adolescence.

Invisible crown on his head.

He is bald now.

Cancer ate away his hair,

and I rubbed Witch Hazel on his foot.

I kissed his forehead.

I am thirteen again and my heart is inexperienced.

I am not ready for the lightening on its way to me.

My hands are too small to hold the weight

of what's about to happen.

What if I choose the wrong thing to do?

she sings,

and during my soldier walks,

the cab driver in a nice suit—

his words are hip like his style

and his commandment, "Don't sleep ready rose,"

meaning: "Don't sleep in your outside clothes."

I feel so lost. I don't know what to do.

In he walks,

tight-roping Yolanda's lyrics in those sharp suits,

riding on the back of my preteen memories,

and I curl my small fingers into a fist

and fit them inside the center of Daddy's palm

the way we used to do.

The way his hand covered my entire fist,

the way he's tight-roping on my heart strings,

the way memory crawled its way into my throat this morning.

I just need to hear one word from you.

Yolanda's voice penetrates the clouds,

the thunder growls,

the lightning strikes,

and I am thirteen again and the year is 2000.

It is the final moan of a passing storm

when James walks out of the door,

his name planting kisses on my forehead

and anointing my eyes

with grief.

LUNGS

The river in my eyes.

The grief under my skin.

I am almost out of breath,

but prayer is a second lung.

ALL OR NOTHING

I don't know how to feel half-heartedly,

how to be passionate sparsely,

how to love raindrops at a time.

I don't know how to half-

shine.

So I apologize.

I am sorry if my sun

burned your skin.

If I came in too hot

or if I am sometimes too cold,

a forest of ice

and long blades of frozen grass

bowing under the weight

of bitter winds.

A breath of vapor,

purple lips,

and chattering teeth.

Yecheilyah Ysrayl

I promise you that

this heart of stone

is really just flesh,

learning to beat one pulse at a time.

Just don't ask me to half-shine.

I don't know how to feel half-heartedly.

I cannot promise not to love you

dangerously,

for I am all

or nothing.

BLACK RAGE

Black rage is the fire of the frustrated outcasts of society.

The superior servants suppressed and robbed of significance.

A hungry lion let loose.

Black rage is the growl of the heavy hearts of the world,

the intensity of *fed-upness* burning hot,

jumping, and howling.

It snarls and bites.

Black rage is a dancing fire,

marching down the street

and wrapping itself around corners.

Black rage is eating everything in its path,

choking clouds of toxic smoke,

an inferno no one notices exists until it bursts.

Black rage is blazing and out of control

from bodies that fell to the ground

Yecheilyah Ysrayl

and left there like dirty flakes of snow.

Black rage is over 400 years of subjugation,

of working years on end with no break.

Black rage is souls exhausted.

It's the disruption that happens

when centuries of silence

speak.

BRAVERY IN INK

Good poetry is bravery in ink.

The audacity to survive without permission,

the exposed spirit,

the sirens of the soul.

Good poetry is naked,

the inward man undisguised.

His words do not ask you to clap,

do not seek for a sign

and only rhyme if they're meant to.

Good poetry does not try to impress you;

its only goal is to speak the truth.

Do not add cream.

Do not add sugar.

Do not water it down.

Take off your clothes

and let the goosebumps tap dance on your skin.

Let the fresh air move through your toes.

Comb your hands through your hair and laugh.

Dance silly,

talk jive,

drink wine,

praise your metaphors.

Write without chains—

There are no slaves here.

Transcribe your heart to the page,

let it bleed,

let it proclaim,

let it sing…

Then you shall know what a good poem is.

Good poetry is bravery in ink.

WHEN THE WORLD LOVES YOU

I hate to have to be the one to tell you this.

After all, you woke up today feeling optimistic, and here I am,

feeding you words that I know you do not want to hear.

But I would not be much of a friend if I didn't tell you

About how the world loves you.

The world will love you after the soil hugs your flesh,

when the breath leaves your body for that place

it will now call home.

The world will bring you home

on the backs of T-Shirts,

on tattoos that kiss flesh,

in a frame on your grandmother's wall

and museums.

It will popularize your name in a post,

speak to you in a language that you will never understand

and in a voice that you will never hear.

Yecheilyah Ysrayl

This is how the world will love you

later.

After the fact,

like they did the Messiah.

It will prop you on their living room walls,

force a crown of thorns around your head,

sacrifice your body to social media

hang you

on their Facebook walls,

hashtag your legacy in cyberspace.

They will celebrate you

like they never did at birth.

I warn you:

They will throw you parties

more significant than anything your eyes ever beheld,

hold you in their memories like a nightmare

from which they cannot awake.

You will haunt them,

and they will love it.

The world will love you in caskets

and in prayers

and tell you secrets in the grave.

They will confide in you

like a man to a woman's hips.

When the world loves you back,

it is in flowers

and candlelight vigils.

It is in marches, street corners, and pictures.

The world will love you in laughter

and in memorials,

in memory and regret.

And I apologize that I have to be the one to tell you this.

After all, you woke up today feeling optimistic,

but I would not be much of a friend if I didn't tell you the truth

about how the world loves you more

in death.

FLESH VS. SPIRIT

My anxiety is loud,

but so is this victory,

so is this freedom,

so is this awakening.

My mind is a warzone

where black and white spirits roam—

both demons and angels alike—

where sorrow and freedom are both soldiers,

fighting for the opportunity to possess me,

to take up space

that is the residence

of my consciousness.

My body is a battlefield

that society tries to sacrifice to its traditions,

and I try not to bleed out

on people who never cut me

36

since I am both spiritual

and fleshly.

So, I shackle myself to my integrity,

being both in chains and free,

enslaved to truth—

a special kind of liberation

submitted

as I strive to overcome this war

between my flesh

and my spirit.

CONTRADICTIONS

If Jesus (as you call him)

was Black (as you call it)

and Jesus was a Jew,

how are the Jews (as you call them)

not Black?

HER BENDED KNEE

Once a mother,

always is

They bend their knees

to raise our kids

They laugh for our broken

as if they never have cried—

for our burden, they soothe,

as if our souls had died

They put up with our demons

on the top of their heads

colored gray with grief,

fake smiles,

and gritted teeth.

A generation held together

by tiny pieces of silver string—

those grayish-white pieces of hair,

a prophesy of her bended knees.

Their bodies ache due to our trials and needs

Our depression states

and our miscarried dreams

all have a home on the top of mother's head.

Our minds, they touch

Our bull, they fed

Can't wash the stench

of our almost dead,

but they straighten their backs

and lift their chins,

throwing on their head

our hopes and sins—

and at night

when we run the streets

and sleep in sheets,

they bend their knee

and cry to sleep

and then wake up

all smiles and grace.

Let us never see tears run down her face

Instead, see your life on your mother's head

the next time you see those

grayish whites

Just know that someone prays for you at night—

no tears are seen,

all frowns are gone,

just bended knees

and prayer songs

GUILTY

I vomit kindness from my gut

and I am overflowing

drowning

in compassion for people

who have none

for me.

Guilty,

I let them swim here

for free.

WILL THERE BE A FIRE NEXT TIME?

Ten years from now,

when you do not see protests on the news;

twenty years from now,

when George Floyd's blood has dried up

and Ahmaud Arbery is nothing more than a Google search,

when you no longer see your brothers and sisters

marching

and protesting in the streets for justice,

thirty years from now,

when there are no more hashtags

on which to hang your consciousness

and no Instagram to snapshot the revolution,

when "black," is no longer trending…

will there be a fire next time?

When the news goes back to its regularly scheduled program

and the American flag is still soaked with the blood of the saints, their memory etched into the concrete we walk on,

who will walk on?

When the history books forget

to mention Breonna Taylor's name, will we?

Did you know there were *five* little girls injured

during the bombing of the 16th Street Baptist Church in 1963?

Did you know that the fifth little girl,

Sarah Collins Rudolph, lived?

Forty years from now, whose legacy lives?

Who will honor Emmett Till and Trayvon Martin's memory?

When America's anger sizzles into complacency,

will there be a fire next time?

SO, SHE SANG POETRY

Poetry was the cry of a caged bird.

Inside, imprisoned by walls, she built herself,

her chest heavy with questions

she did not have the guts to ask

She felt her voice was too secret,

her mission too silent,

her purpose too underground railroad—

and ain't nobody wanna be free.

So she sang poetry,

and the walls melted like liquid honey.

It was startling how her voice vibrated the air

and she saw her skeletons, ugly and raw,

a graveyard of insecurities locked inside the cages of her mind

She was not dead, but something else was…

She saw the struggles of her voice,

the agony of a quiet storm in a world full of noise.

45

Yecheilyah Ysrayl

Her mind was a Civil War,

and she wasn't sure who would win:

the enslaved or the free

So, she sang poetry

and the shackles melted like liquid honey.

There was strength in her lungs,

she could not tame the lyric

There was no trapping the soul,

no caging the courage,

no binding the song.

There was freedom in her fingers

and a revolution in her pen.

Paper was a bloodbath of truth

and writing a sanctuary.

Fear did not live here,

only wings that lifted her above the ground

A canvas of silver linings across the sky,

a colorful reminder that her struggles

were stepping-stones

to freedom,

that her flaws were flawless

and her mistakes, miracles in disguise

These were her confessions,

a resurrection

written in ink.

Poetry was the cry of a caged bird

who learned to sing poetry

until the bars melted away

like liquid honey.

ABORTED PURPOSE

I know too many women aborting their purpose.

We're manipulating our daughters

so that their dreams

are tied to two horses

and the Black family unit is pulled apart.

And we watch as our sons Willie Lynch their seeds

on Fallopian tubes

and then walk away.

They forgot what grew there.

They forgot there are trees within their DNA.

But we gave birth to boys who never became men.

I know too many women aborting their purpose.

We forgot the generations of women

we carried in our ovaries at conception,

so we miscarried Eve's redemption,

now the hand-me-down fabric of expired womanhood

dangling over the degrees of our bedroom walls.

We traded our integrity for dried ink on top cream-colored paper,

the folded crease and stained remembrance of what we used to be

before the glass ceiling defined us,

the faded glory of the Black family unit,

before we were Divas and Bosses,

back in the day when we were content being Queens.

We traded our crowns in exchange

to do bad all by ourselves

Now there's the stress

and the guilt

of 70% of Black women

whose descendants will stare down

the barrel of a gun

because she could not admit

that it takes more than a Black mother

to raise

a Black son.

BEAUTY

You are so beautiful

when you are yourself.

There is nothing

more gorgeous

than this.

TILL WHEN?

I heard a child's voice

come from the mouth of an older woman.

Then, another until there were four.

Four child voices from four elderly women.

Then I realized that the older women were not elderly;

They had child voices because they had died as children.

Four Little Girls are still trying to tear down

the bricks

painted on the sides of their heads.

Pocket-book scriptures are still hanging

from underneath their tongues.

That 15th of September

in the 1963rd year of their Lord,

like a scorched covenant under burned fingernails

still waiting for me to remember,

they asked me if Martin was still dreaming,

Yecheilyah Ysrayl

And the trauma in their face

that came next

knocked me off my feet.

His brains caught somewhere alongside somebody's cotton gin,

genitals scattered alongside somebody's river,

frightened my bones.

A burst of a laughter more frightening

than decomposed bodies

at the bottom of biracial rivers whispered

like the voice of Emmett:

"Till when?" he asked me.

Then strings of voices erupted from someplace

beyond the banks of the James River,

from some time before Willie Lynch's arrival,

somewhere marching

and stomping on my roots.

Somewhere printed on the back of the forbidden fruit

I still got between my teeth,

a string of voices sprung up from the oppression,

marching down the streets of Birmingham,

Chicago,

Mississippi,

Harlem

Willie Edwards,

James Chaney,

Michael Donald,

Michael Griffith,

Michael Brown,

Yusef Hawkings,

Eric Gardner,

George Floyd,

Ahmaud Arbery,

James Byrd Jr. and Trayvon Martin's voices sang hymns
of "I told you so's," like women giving birth to stillborn children.

"Till when?" they asked me.
"Will you people continue to give birth to death
still lying on the bed of Martin's dreams?"

Yecheilyah Ysrayl

They sang with authority

like rolling thunder

and butterflies in my stomach.

Like truth on top Moses mountain, they sang.

Like Earthquakes, they sang.

Like blood-thirsty whales behind slave ships.

Like ripping flesh torn open

with Hebrew scriptures in its veins, they sang.

Like diseases written in the sky and prison chains,

their voices roared like a million "I told you so's."

They sang as voices do,

and they asked me a question,

but their words were few.

"Till when?"

STUDY THE ART

Why should anyone trust me

with the responsibility of poetry

if I know nothing

of the poets

who came

before me?

A MAN

I knew I would marry someone like him

when I saw my dad's skin crawl away from his bones,

his soul castrated,

the angel of death standing over his head

shouting cancer in the loudest whisper I had ever heard,

bouncing off the walls of our apartment home.

I knew the kind of person I would marry

the day my father's breath got up and left,

did not take me with it

and left nothing

but

the definition

of a man.

QUEASY

Change is a sickly feeling.

Your stomach reels and gurgles,

threatening to spill waves of vomit

from the belly of a future unknown.

And yet, I know the power of self-examination

of mirrors and light:

they will require me to change

or let go completely.

How do I reject what once felt

as close as the breath in my mouth?

How will I lay this burden down?

The conclusion of what has been

for what will be

Who knew new beginnings could be so

queasy...

METAMORPHOSIS

The corners of her pride reach for the floor

and she pulls it back annd tucks it in,

wrapping herself in the cocoon that is her reproach.

It may as well be winter because she is freezing.

Cold. Internally numb.

Goosebumps even grow on the top of her skin.

And even though it is warm outside,

her teeth chatter.

She pulls her legs up against her chest,

resting her head on her knees

and rocking.

The room is dark; the curtains are drawn up.

They call it depression,

but they do not know that she will be beautiful soon.

That her reproach will turn into rejoicing,

her moans into praise,

her cries into courage,

her test into testimonies,

and her weakness into strength.

They do not know that she will have wings, and she will fly.

They do not know that she is a pupa, a full-grown caterpillar,

protected inside a cocoon of silk to develop her power,

growing uncomfortably, changing shape,

and morphing

into a butterfly.

PRAY

—— ❧ ——

When your head is down,

pray.

You are already

bowed.

HIS SKIN

Handsome does not conjure the strength

succulent enough

to uncover the sun underneath his skin.

Shame on those who sexualize him,

who see his body as cheap and public.

Who does he think he is,

being darker than a brown paper bag?

Sometimes they notice him,

like the sun swinging in the sky—

and still, he is only handsome for a *dark-skinned* guy.

They do not know that he is the color of the gods.

I'd describe him as the intensity of ebony,

a precious rarity.

How'd he get so lucky?

Who bathed him in sunlight?

This black hardwood-colored flesh,

delicately bronzed.

He is black keys on a piano.

Play a song for me.

Whisper truth through lips

thick and sensual,

remarkably soft and pliable.

This espresso-colored body.

Dangerous when diluted.

Potent when raw.

They do not know any better.

How do you greet someone so breathtakingly gorgeous?

It will take them a minute to get used to the truth—

That not even the bite of winter

can dare diminish

his light.

LESSONS

I learned that denying a part of myself

to fit in does nothing but break me

into pieces—

And here I am, a scrambled egg,

a mess of egg yolk

that does not belong.

And I learned that holding onto people

who would never hold onto me,

does nothing but make me

bleed.

And I learned

this is not

healing…

TWO HEARTS

Somewhere in time,

where my locs are sterling tree branches

and your beard a whitish grey,

two stars shining in opposite ends of the Universe,

two pillars of light,

two hearts pulled together like magnets,

two souls connecting like magic…

Of this, I am certain:

I will love you *forever*.

AND THIS IS WINNING

Hope stopped holding its breath that day.

It settled in the pit of her stomach.

She could taste the give-up on her tongue,

feel the despair like plaque on her teeth.

There was something wrong with her place in the world.

Even then (even at ten),

she knew that she was different.

What is worse than a little girl displaced?

A little girl who *understands* her displacement

of knowing too much.

Too much ache,

Too much suffering,

Too much pain,

Too much ignorance,

Too much knowing and not knowing at the same time,

Too much internal confusion.

Yecheilyah Ysrayl

She did not know that she could be

in the world, but not *of* it,

so she opted to take herself *out* of it.

Nothing was more certain

than that expected end

and the relief her mind held

of being free.

But then,

the hope grew

unexpectedly,

shockingly,

miraculously.

A glint of light, a spark of life,

like wings had grown

out of what was left of her spine.

Hope blossomed,

and these thoughts of suicide died.

And this little girl turned eleven

and twelve,

then woman

and taught

and teaches

and wrote

and writes

and hopes

and has faith

and is strong.

And this

is

winning…

OUR CHILDREN

You are fourteen,

and despite the infantile laughter—

the one gentler than the fresh coat of love

on a baby's skin—

your mothers must warn you

that certain skin tones won't allow you

to flash open innocence.

You are not allowed to purchase candy,

eat ice cream,

tell jokes, jog,

or fall in love with cream-colored coffee.

Or show your strength in the open hallways of street corners.

Do not point your skin in the direction of authority.

Do not showcase your power in the open air, my sons.

Do not boast in the black pearls radiating from your smiles,

my daughters.

Hide your treasured possessions

until it is time for them to be fulfilled.

Specific histories won't let you forget the present

or permit childhood to take advantage of your fingerprints.

Responsibilities follow you home

in warm booties, blankets, and prophecies.

If only you had known that your existence

would give birth to a movement,

if you only had known that your delivery

would echo the sounds of captivity

long before your feet hit the ground.

Before your mother's pelvis danced against your fathers,

and his kiss brushed upon her skin...

Did they tell you that you were born for this?

Did they tell you about the cries of Israel

when they reached into the heavens like hands

just as heavy as your parent's hearts,

knocking against the doors of heaven

because too many of their prayers ended in question marks?

Yecheilyah Ysrayl

Did they tell you that you were destined to die?

That you had final movement stamped to your backside

like a receipt back to the soil.

Like your fathers had to spit their seed into a melody,

an Amazing Grace and Birmingham Sunday,

carving its lyrics and your names into the history books

of our yet unborn.

And while you rest,

they march scripture on the bed

of your misunderstood self.

CONSEQUENCES OF A LONELY HEART

The thought arose at midnight.

Somewhere between the witching hours of deception

and the sparkling thighs that rubbed away

what was left

of her common sense.

It waited for her to open herself up,

so that the incarceration of her heart

can be weighed

against the gold of her patience.

She could not have been less wise

back when she let exploitation play its numbers on her skin,

like melting pearls sliding down the creases

of a well-worn backbone

that she traded in for a brief moment

of Black Orchard

or Issel Miyake cologne.

Though neither could wash away the shame

to which lust had gifted

her thoughts

and now, her soul.

A witness to the tragedy of rose petals aligning the secret bath

where she has mixed in her cup of distorted priorities

that now only smelled like death.

In becoming one with another,

she failed to become herself.

HURTING HIM TAUGHT HER HOW TO LOVE

For years, she could not say his name out loud;

could not accept that she was the villain

in the stories he would one day tell his wife;

could not accept she was the devil

in his life

How had she become such a monster?

It tortured her to think her name was now

among the list of women he regretted knowing.

There are love poems about women like her.

Women who fall in love with men

before falling in love with themselves first,

then leave the men hopeless

or hanging on by strings.

As much as she hurt him,

it hurt her twice as much,

and yet breaking him taught her

how to love another.

She learned to cherish masculinity.

Learned how to hold it in her hands

with all its precious roar

and lion teeth.

No one is always the victim,

and she is not the innocent person she thought she was,

but now she understands how to value love

because there is no pain equivalent to that of breaking

a man.

MIRACLES

How am I still healthy?

All this trauma,

this internal turmoil

of past and present and therapy…

Does this body need treatment?

Is this a soul hurt?

Am I still alive?

How am I still alive?

I have been trying to leave pity in someone else's cup

and the taste of bitterness in someone else's mouth

because heaviness is a thief.

It comes and goes with or without permission,

but the sadness cannot live here.

Not here with me,

not with my healthy self.

And I wonder:

Yecheilyah Ysrayl

How am I not immune

from all this anguish,

all this feeling?

How did I come out of it… *full?*

How did I get so… *whole?*

How am I still healthy?

How am I still standing?

This, too, is a miracle.

ON SACRED GROUND

We planted songs in cotton fields.

backs bent low

with pain in our toes and heels.

Our voices prayed when we could not.

A historical document born underneath our tongues,

they called it a spiritual when we planted songs

on sacred ground.

Hope sprang from the calluses on our thumbs,

watched as *Massa* sold our sons,

packed up freedom in the Mississippi dirt,

moved up North where pain didn't hurt.

Silly us, couldn't let it be…

Thought strange fruit only grew on Southern Trees.

So, we traded our crowns in for concrete,

stopped growing our food to buy our meat.

Insects we purchased for rats,

Yecheilyah Ysrayl

gave up the land

for the projects.

Community tight, though enslaved we were

Gave up the property to call him "Sir."

But in the words of the old folk:

"All that glitter ain't gold."

Just because you don't see chains

don't mean you ain't sold.

Stay true to yourself, to your history, your roots.

Let no one come along and steal your truth.

Pay attention to what's real and what is sound,

and keep your feet rooted

on sacred ground.

NO ONE TALKS ABOUT HOW HARD FAITH IS

No one talks about how laborious faith is.

How mentally challenging it is to wait for something

that feels like it is never going to come,

and believe it is still yours.

To see without seeing.

Seeing beyond sight.

No one talks about the exhaustion

that comes with seeing the beauty where there is none.

To begin again and not feel silly for surrendering to strength.

To keep falling and getting up again.

Each time, being strong but feeling weak.

Each time knowing that what is easy is not worth it

and what is hard is worth everything.

No one talks about what it's like to hold on to hope,

even as it is slipping through your fingers.

Yecheilyah Ysrayl

To faith-walk the staircase with no idea what's at the top.

To believe that you can see, even when you can't.

To believe you are not standing alone, even when you are.

To foresight your way to the next step.

To be future and present at the same time.

To act according to what's coming and not just what is here.

No one talks about the mental fortitude it takes

to be patient and still

and to see nothing and everything

at the same time.

INTEGRITY

I dislike this day and age

where everyone wants to be seen and praised and prized.

Purposely present to spew pillars of knowledge

that is pulled and preserved for a time.

No one wants to be silent,

but everyone wants to be wise.

So, we *selfie* our way into stardom on the ground.

No one wants to stand behind the curtain

or risk being forgotten,

or admit that integrity is doing what's right,

even when no one is looking.

WHY WRITERS SHOULD KEEP WRITING

Not everyone will broadcast to the world

how your vulnerability saved their life.

How they silently depend on the wisdom of your words,

like pieces of salvation scribbled in ink.

Some people are thirsty to hear your voice,

and they wait for you to gather the courage

to wrap them in that red cape we call writing.

They are waiting for you to make them heroes

to whatever suffering led them here.

Not everyone is looking for words that are pretty either,

cute, cuddly, and attractive looking.

Some people need not be coddled,

but scorned out of comfort zones

and disciplined out of negligence.

Writers should keep writing

because they are saviors

to people they may never know.

OPPOSITES ATTRACT

They were nothing alike, but just the same.

The connection scared her

because he knew her thoughts before she did.

He was inside of her, and they had not even touched.

He brought out the fight,

the wild,

the lioness,

the roar,

the *freak*, even.

He was air

and it felt like freedom.

MOURNING

I do not hear the thunder growl.

I do not see the flash of light.

I do not know what the trigger is,

but tears come like unexpected rain.

No sympathy in the world will curve this hunger.

It is years after the diagnosis,

and the melanin in my skin cannot hide the redness of my cheeks.

There is no name for this feeling,

no real way to describe this emptiness.

Scorched that parenthood snaked its way through my fingers,

and robbed me of this fairy-tale.

There is no escaping the innocence flooding my timelines.

This laughing womb—

It mocks my audacity to dream,

and I am standing here drenched in water.

Cold. Numb. Without feeling.

Yecheilyah Ysrayl

No words.

My tongue clings to the roof of my mouth.

What is there to say when I can barely move my legs?

All this talk of motherhood,

and I pretend not to feel absent,

to be present and not fall apart from shame.

I am a master at pretending that

seeing you mothering

does not hurt me.

Because it is years after the diagnosis,

and the melanin in my skin cannot hide the redness of my cheeks.

Only prayer can silence the aching

of this mourning.

THE LITTLE THINGS

I like poems.

Side-aching laughter.

Traveling.

Museums.

Spirited conversation.

Text messages.

French vanilla flavored coffee.

I like music.

Courageous hearts.

Wine.

Rain.

Books.

Intimacy.

I like soul.

DO NOT TELL ME YOU KNOW WHAT STRENGTH IS

If you have never

been depressed,

curled your body into the fetal position

or cried rivers into your fists,

then do not tell me you know

what strength is.

QUIETUDE

Silence laughs at the foolishness

of our impatience.

How we hurry to disrupt the quietude,

and only end up sick with questions

and fishing for a thought.

What is the next move to be made in the stillness?

What revelation taps against the calm meditations of the heart?

What revolution for our cries?

What reproof must we seek to understand

in the devastating muteness of the air?

SENSITIVE SOUL

Brutally honest.

Brutally sensitive.

Not a saint,

just a sensitive soul

with a conscious.

CRY OUT

How does it make you feel

to see someone mistreating themselves;

to hear them poison their mouth with self-hate language;

to disrespect their soul with insecurities?

Do your intestines not cringe?

Do they not wrap themselves around the wrongness there?

The diseased spirit of a person defeated.

Does your stomach not turn into knots?

Does the human in you not cry out?

Imagine if you were observing yourself doing the same:

Poisoning your mouth with self-hate language

and disrespecting your soul with insecurities.

Do your intestines not cringe?

Do they not wrap themselves around the wrongness there?

Do you recognize the diseased spirit of *this* person defeated?

Does your stomach turn into knots?

Yecheilyah Ysrayl

When you are self-hating yourself,

does the human in you

cry out?

DEAR DECEPTION

You try to hide, but I know you are there.

I can hear it when they walk and smell it in their smiles.

The truth is that you inebriate them with lies,

overflowing their presence like air under pressure.

It's a shame that some of them can't even stand up straight,

staggering through social media,

unaware that their ignorance is showing.

You have taught them to expose their nakedness.

Now their heart is blackened with the scars of falsehood,

and their minds poisoned with comfort.

Sometimes, they are even unaware of the stench they carry

like walking viruses and destructive pestilence.

They sit among graves and befriend

the first corpse

they see smiling.

You think you know wisdom,

but foolishness is bathed in your shadow,

and kindness is a game you play on the weak's minds,

snickering behind the concocted words of flattery

and the secret winking you perform under the mask you wear.

You have fallen prey to your own fabricated illusions,

casting manipulating spells on the unknown,

yet you wrap yourself in white and wear a silver wig.

Indeed, you are deception,

a lie that is made to look like

the truth.

POETRY

Poetry is my husband's scent

and my mother's smile.

FOR THOSE WHO ARE SAD

Can I cradle you in the nook of my arms?

If you were here, would you let me?

Hold you, I mean.

I don't just want a hug;

I want to hold you, so we cry together.

Kiss the top of your forehead like a mother would.

On the shoulder of comfort, let your tears drench my shirt,

and I will love you like an infant.

Can these words hold your head up?

I do not want the soft spot of your pain

to blemish the fragile newness of the warrior you are becoming.

Your critics will look at what you are,

but I see what you can become.

But you've got to let me do my job.

Let me hold you.

Cradle you in my arms with these words.

Cradle you in my arms with this pen.

This is not a book.

No, not today.

Today this is air.

This is breath.

This is permission to breathe.

These are words wooing lullabies

for the exhausted spirits of the broken.

THE BEAUTIFUL AND THE BROKEN

To the addicted,

To the drunkards,

To the prostitutes,

To the lonely,

To the depressed,

To the sad,

To the homeless,

To the hungry,

To the lowly,

To the lame,

To the dumb,

To the *weirdos*, and the awkward ones,

To the *uneducated*,

To the heartbroken,

To the misunderstood,

To those who are crazy,

and to those who are poor,

you are loved.

You are balance.

For what is appreciation without loss?

What is joy without sorrow?

What is healing without suffering?

What is life without death?

You are the perfect combination

of the beautiful

and the broken.

Please, stay.

ON SOFT HEARTS

Please do not ask us not to care.

We will care anyway.

We will wonder why the flower doesn't bloom,

why its petals are dry.

Why is there a flower falling to pieces for lack of moisture?

We will wonder about the soil and the colors in the sky.

We will mourn with those who are sad

and rub empathy on those who are bruised.

We will care about people

who probably won't think twice about us.

We will take this heart of flesh

and show them that we are hurt too

and we too have been trampled upon.

Here, see the holes and scars on our skin.

But this doesn't mean we have to let our hearts grow cold.

We do not have to build walls that are too high for people to climb.

When everyone's a savage, do not be afraid to be soft.

There has to be someone in this chaotic world

who can show proof that there can still be love

after war.

THERAPY

No one can tell me

that writing is not

therapy.

2020

2020 has taught us that we are not in control.

But hindsight is 2020, so this, we do not yet know.

AWAKENING

Awakened from a slumber of lies,

where I stood baptized in tradition's rebellion.

Unplugged from the matrix,

where I drowned intoxicated by the signs of the times.

Power in my soul.

Purpose in my bones.

Prophecies birthmarked on the top of my skin.

A second resurrection to offset my sins.

A second chance to be born.

A new spirit awakens.

WHEN THE SILENCE SPEAKS

Silence says what words cannot.

So then, how do you discern the quiet?

Decipher the stillness?

Disentangle the hush?

You don't.

You sit with the thought.

You *feel* the feeling.

You embrace the confusion

and laugh at the pain.

You sit there, and you ache or mourn, or praise, or cry.

You sit there, mute, and let the quiet do its job.

If you embrace the tranquility of the moment,

you might emerge a Maya Angelou

and unearth the most profound revelations

when the silence speaks.

THERE IS MOVEMENT IN STILLNESS

I saw a sunflower bow to a bee without moving.

It arched its stem, its petals already stretched wide and willing.

There it waited for the wind to whistle;

the way it does when it pushes the flower forward,

and here, the flower bowed.

Beautiful and with grace,

this sunflower let itself go in the wind's direction,

its sweet substance carrying the scent of fresh Nectar.

I couldn't smell it, but it wasn't for me to smell,

so I looked down in my notebook and wrote a reminder:

"What is for you is for you."

I looked up and noticed a bumblebee singing its way to our area.

But the flower did not move, it waited.

The wind only moved the flower—

the invisible force that guides it.

So I wrote in my notebook:

"Do not chase, attract.

What is yours will come to you.

Put out the right scent

and let the invisible force guide you."

I looked up, and the bee seemed much more anxious

and excited,

but I knew better than to kill it.

This creature was on a mission,

so I didn't swat him away because this wasn't my business.

I was here only as a witness

to this meditative buzz of togetherness.

I saw a sunflower bow to a bee without moving,

and I bowed my head and wrote:

"There is a movement even in stillness."

Thank you for reading my book!

It would mean a great deal to me if you could give me your opinion by leaving an honest review. Not only will this let me know how you feel about my writing in general, but potential readers will also value your feedback.

You can also shoot me an email at yecheilyah@yecheilyahysrayl.com